CROCODILES

Please visit our web site at: www.garethstevens.com
For a free color catalog describing Gareth Stevens Publishing's
list of high-quality books and multimedia programs, call
1-800-542-2595 (USA) or 1-800-387-3178 (Canada).
Gareth Stevens Publishing's fax: (414) 332-3567.

All about crocodiles.
    Crocodiles.
        p. cm. — (All about wild animals)
    Previously published in Great Britain as: All about crocodiles. 2002.
    ISBN 0-8368-4182-4 (lib. bdg.)
        1. Crocodiles—Juvenile literature. I. Title. II. Series.
    QL666.C925A568   2004
    597.98'2—dc22   2004040814

This edition first published in 2005 by
Gareth Stevens Publishing
A World Almanac Education Group Company
330 West Olive Street, Suite 100
Milwaukee, Wisconsin 53212 USA

This U.S. edition copyright © 2005 by Gareth Stevens, Inc. Original edition
copyright © 2002 by DeAgostini UK Limited. First published in 2002 as
My Animal Kingdom: All About Crocodiles by DeAgostini UK Ltd., Griffin House,
161 Hammersmith Road, London W6 8SD, England. Additional end matter
copyright © 2005 by Gareth Stevens, Inc.

Editorial and design: Tucker Slingsby Ltd., London
Gareth Stevens series editor: Catherine Gardner
Gareth Stevens art direction: Tammy West

Picture Credits
NHPA — Martin Harvey: Front cover, title page, 8–9, 14, 15, 15, 16, 18, 18–19,
        20, 23; Anthony Bannister: 9; Christophe Ratier: 12; Daniel Heuclin: 13;
        Steve Robinson: 19; Karl Switak: 24; E. A. Janes: 27; Jonathan and Angela
        Scott: 28–29.
Oxford Scientific Films — Mark Deeble and Victoria Stone: 7, 13, 17, 21, 24–25;
        Joe McDonald: 22; ABPL Photo Library: 23; Michael Fogden: 26;
        Richard Packwood: 27; Mike Price/SAL: 27; Okapia: 28.
© Joe McDonald/Visuals Unlimited: 6-7
Artwork — Black Hat: 11.

Printed in the United States of America

1 2 3 4 5 6 7 8 9 08 07 06 05 04

CROCODILES

Gareth Stevens Publishing
A WORLD ALMANAC EDUCATION GROUP COMPANY

CROCODILE FACTS

ANIMAL GROUP: reptile

COLOR: dark green to brownish black on top with a lighter colored belly

SIZE: up to 20 feet (6 meters) long from the head to the tip of the tail

WEIGHT: as much as 2,205 pounds (1,000 kilograms), or about the same weight as a small car

SPEED: up to 9 miles (14 kilometers) per hour when running on land

EATS: meat

DRINKS: water

LIVES: up to 100 years

Words that appear in the glossar are printed in **boldface** type the first time they occur in the text.

CONTENTS

A Closer Look 6

Home, Sweet Home 10

Neighbors 12

The Family 14

Life on Land 18

Favorite Foods 20

Danger! 22

A Crocodile's Day 24

Relatives 26

Humans and Crocodiles 28

Glossary 30

Index 32

A CLOSER LOOK

A crocodile is a large, lizard-shaped **reptile** with four short legs and a long, strong tail. Crocodiles are the largest reptiles on Earth. One kind of crocodile, known as the Nile crocodile, is as long and as heavy as a small car! Like all reptiles, a crocodile has scales covering its body. Big, bony scales with ridges protect its back. Smoother scales cover its belly. Unlike other reptiles, a crocodile does not **molt**. A crocodile's skin grows with its body.

DID YOU KNOW?

- The word *crocodile* means "lizard of the Nile."

- The Nile is a river that flows through eastern Africa. The Nile — the longest river in the world — is 4,160 miles (6,695 kilometers) long.

I have tough scales for protection.

My powerful tail helps me swim.

My hind feet are webbed.

SLEEK SWIMMERS

Crocodiles swim using their huge, oarlike tails. When they swim slowly, they steer with their legs and feet. When they swim fast, crocodiles tuck their legs into their sides.

On land, I can use my short, strong legs to walk and even to run.

I have long jaws with lots of sharp teeth.

A crocodile's eyes, ears, and nostrils are on the top of its head, so a crocodile can see, hear, and breathe while its body is underwater. Crocodiles have sharp senses to help them find and catch food. Crocodiles are dangerous **predators** that have hunted **prey** in much the same way for almost 200 million years!

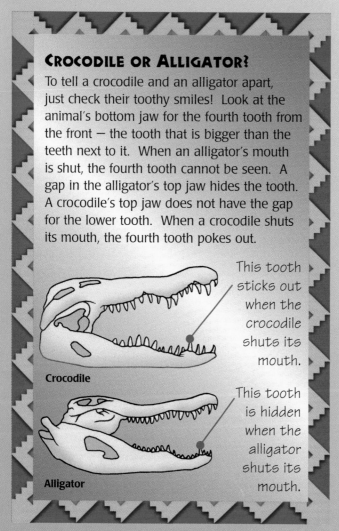

CROCODILE OR ALLIGATOR?

To tell a crocodile and an alligator apart, just check their toothy smiles! Look at the animal's bottom jaw for the fourth tooth from the front — the tooth that is bigger than the teeth next to it. When an alligator's mouth is shut, the fourth tooth cannot be seen. A gap in the alligator's top jaw hides the tooth. A crocodile's top jaw does not have the gap for the lower tooth. When a crocodile shuts its mouth, the fourth tooth pokes out.

This tooth sticks out when the crocodile shuts its mouth.

Crocodile

This tooth is hidden when the alligator shuts its mouth.

Alligator

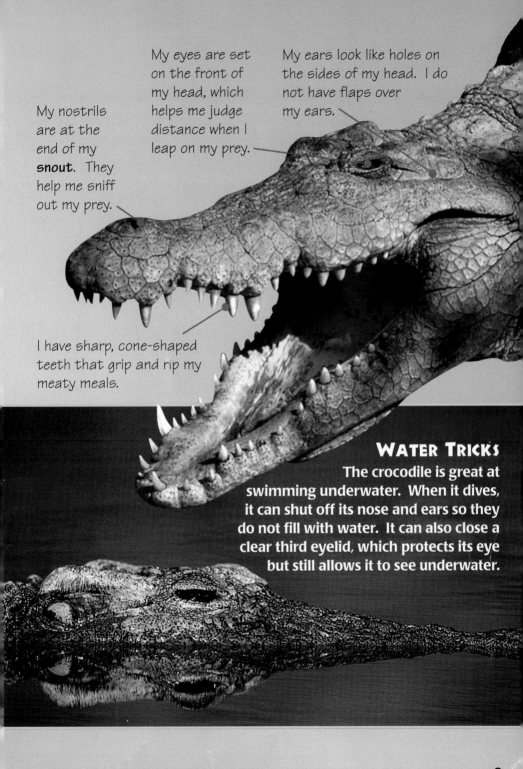

My nostrils are at the end of my **snout**. They help me sniff out my prey.

My eyes are set on the front of my head, which helps me judge distance when I leap on my prey.

My ears look like holes on the sides of my head. I do not have flaps over my ears.

I have sharp, cone-shaped teeth that grip and rip my meaty meals.

WATER TRICKS

The crocodile is great at swimming underwater. When it dives, it can shut off its nose and ears so they do not fill with water. It can also close a clear third eyelid, which protects its eye but still allows it to see underwater.

Home, Sweet Home

Nile crocodiles live in the Nile River, of course, and in many other rivers and lakes in Africa. They spend a lot of time in the water. In the wet season, the rivers flood, so the crocodiles can hunt in a bigger area than usual. In the dry season, the rivers return to a normal level, and the crocodiles go back to their river homes.

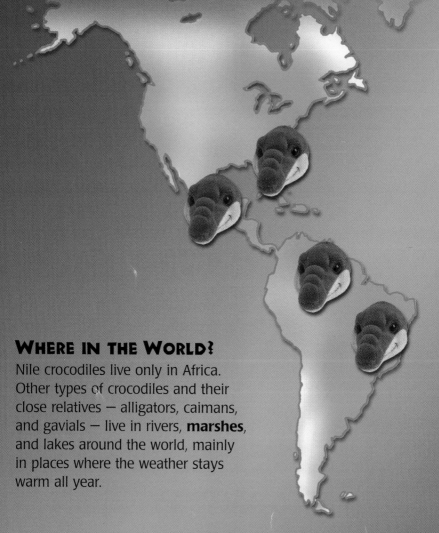

Where in the World?

Nile crocodiles live only in Africa. Other types of crocodiles and their close relatives — alligators, caimans, and gavials — live in rivers, **marshes**, and lakes around the world, mainly in places where the weather stays warm all year.

DID YOU KNOW?

- The first crocodiles lived almost 200 million years ago, at the same time as dinosaurs.

- Crocodiles are the closest living relatives of the dinosaurs. Both dinosaurs and crocodiles belong to a group of animals known as Archosauria.

- Deinosuchus, or the "terror crocodile," was the biggest crocodile ever known. It was about 50 feet (15 meters) long.

BIG BROTHER

The saltwater crocodile is the biggest living reptile in the world. It can grow to be more than 23 feet (7 m) long and weigh as much as ten people! The saltwater crocodile lives along the ocean coasts of southeastern Asia and Australia.

NEIGHBORS

Rivers in **tropical** parts of the world are always warm and full of wildlife. Nile crocodiles share their river homes with thousands of fish, frogs, birds, and snakes. Other animals, such as antelopes, lions, zebras, and giraffes, visit the river to drink or take a bath. Crocodiles are not the friendliest animals in the river neighborhood. Many of a crocodile's neighbors also are the crocodile's prey!

MARSH DWELLER

The sitatunga is a shy antelope that grazes on marsh plants. It has a striped coat to help it hide among the **reeds** and huge hooves to help it walk on wet ground without sinking.

NILE NEIGHBOR

A Nile soft-shelled turtle may look cute when it hatches, but it grows up to be a hungry predator. As it swims through the water, it looks for fish and frogs to eat. The Nile soft-shelled turtle has the perfect **adaptations** for its watery life. It can breathe through its lungs and its soft shell. It also has webbed feet for speedy swimming.

BIG BEAK

A shoebill is a rare large blue-gray stork. Its big boat-shaped bill scoops up food from the water. It usually eats fish, frogs, and young turtles, but a shoebill can scoop up a baby crocodile if it gets a chance.

THE FAMILY

Up to one hundred crocodiles live together in a group, but the crocodiles in the group leave each other alone. Each of the biggest male crocodiles in the group guards its own **territory**. The big males keep smaller males from taking their mates or their food. To send messages to the other members of their group, crocodiles use certain kinds of sounds and body movements.

Like most reptiles, crocodiles start their lives as eggs. A female crocodile lays from twenty-five to ninety-five white, hard-shelled eggs in a nest she digs in the riverbank. She covers the eggs with plants and sand and guards the nest for the next three months. As the eggs start to open, the **hatchlings** make chirping sounds. The female uncovers the nest and carries the babies to the river in her mouth.

KEEP AWAY!

Male crocodiles do not like to get too close together! If two males meet, they can tell each other to move by raising their heads, opening their jaws, and growling. Two males that get too close may fight.

EGG TOOTH

It is not easy for a baby crocodile to break out of its egg, but it does have a built-in tool to help. On the top of its nose is a hard area of skin called an egg tooth. A baby crocodile rubs its egg tooth on the inside of its egg to weaken the shell. Then the baby pushes hard with its snout to break through the shell.

BABY FILE

BIRTH

When Nile crocodiles are born, they are about 10 inches (25 centimeters) long. Their striped skins help them hide in the plants and shadows along the river. Their main foods are insects and small fish.

THREE MONTHS

Young crocodiles grow quickly. They add about 12 inches (30 cm) each year. Little crocodiles stay close to their mothers and each other. The world is a dangerous place for crocodile hatchlings. Many of them die before they become adults.

ONE TO TWO YEARS

The young crocodiles gobble up fish, shellfish, and even small **mammals**. By the time they are two years old, their mothers no longer look after them. Instead, they live with crocodiles about their own size. Bigger crocodiles might eat them!

LIFE ON LAND

Crocodiles are cold-blooded, which means they depend on the conditions around them to cool or warm their bodies. They can rest in the river to cool off and sunbathe on the riverbank to warm up. Crocodiles may seem clumsy and slow on land, but they can run as fast as a person.

BIG BURROW

If the weather is too cold or too hot and dry, Nile crocodiles hide. To escape the weather, a group of crocodiles use their claws and snouts to dig a big **burrow** in a muddy riverbank. They remain in the burrow until better weather arrives.

CROCODILE WALK

To move around on land, a crocodile can belly crawl, high walk, or gallop. When a crocodile does a belly crawl, it pushes its legs out to the sides so its chest, stomach, and tail stay flat on the ground. In a high walk (*below*) and in a gallop, a crocodile uses its legs to hold its body off the ground. Crocodiles can gallop at speeds of up to 9 miles (14 km) per hour, but they cannot keep up their top speed for long distances.

CROCODILE SMILE

Crocodiles with their mouths wide open may be ready to take a big bite of food, or they may be sunbathing (*bottom*)! Crocodiles often rest in the Sun with their mouths wide open to soak up the warmth. That big mouth also helps a crocodile cool down or warn enemies to stay away.

FAVORITE FOODS

Crocodiles are crafty predators. They wait at the edge of a river or lake. Only their eyes and nostrils show above the water. They are so still that they look like old logs. When prey comes near — snap! They pull their prey underwater, drown it, and rip off pieces of meat to swallow. Crocodiles have lots of teeth, but they cannot chew.

DID YOU KNOW?

- If a crocodile loses a tooth, it does not worry. It just grows a new one!

- A crocodile swallows little stones, which help grind up the food in its **gut**.

- A flap of skin can cover the opening of a crocodile's throat so it can open its mouth underwater without choking.

WATCH OUT!

Impalas often drink water during the hottest time of day while most predators, such as lions, are resting. A crocodile does not miss a chance at lunch. It lies still until a prey animal is within its reach. Then it leaps out of the water and grabs its prey.

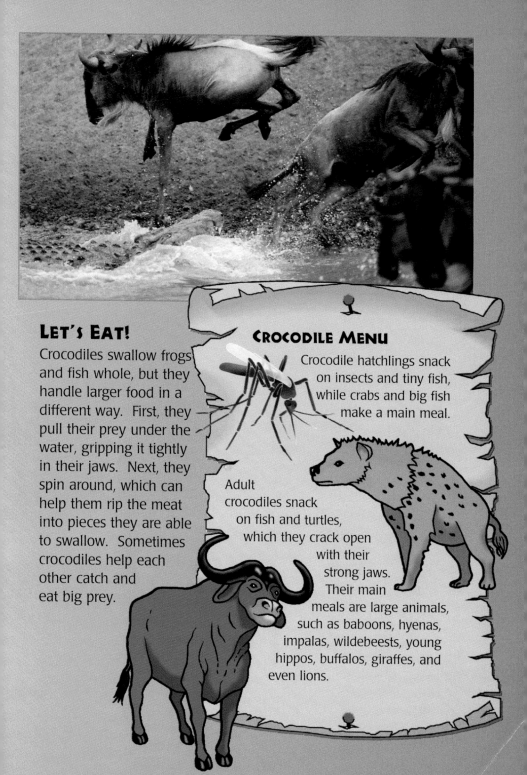

LET'S EAT!

Crocodiles swallow frogs and fish whole, but they handle larger food in a different way. First, they pull their prey under the water, gripping it tightly in their jaws. Next, they spin around, which can help them rip the meat into pieces they are able to swallow. Sometimes crocodiles help each other catch and eat big prey.

CROCODILE MENU

Crocodile hatchlings snack on insects and tiny fish, while crabs and big fish make a main meal.

Adult crocodiles snack on fish and turtles, which they crack open with their strong jaws. Their main meals are large animals, such as baboons, hyenas, impalas, wildebeests, young hippos, buffalos, giraffes, and even lions.

DANGER!

Most often, adult crocodiles are the predators, not the prey! They have few enemies. The worst enemies of crocodiles and alligators are humans who hunt them for their meat and their skins. Crocodile eggs and hatchlings have more enemies to fear. Plenty of hungry predators are happy to gobble them up.

The muscles a crocodile uses to close its jaws are strong. A crocodile can snap its mouth closed with deadly force. On the other hand, the muscles it uses to open its jaws are very weak. A rubber band is all it takes to hold shut the jaws of a 7-foot (2 m) crocodile!

EGG THIEF

The Nile monitor is a big lizard that grows up to 7 feet (2 m) long. This predator eats anything that fits into its mouth. It feasts on unprotected crocodile hatchlings. If it can find a crocodile nest, it steals the eggs and cracks them open to eat the yolks.

WINGED HUNTER

The fish eagle is built to kill. Its eyesight is so sharp that it can spot prey swimming underwater. It has strong claws for gripping its victim and a sharp, hooked bill for tearing flesh. The fish eagle usually hunts fish, but it eats turtles, birds, and young crocodiles, too.

MARSH MONGOOSE

The marsh mongoose is good at swimming and diving — and finding a meal of crocodile eggs. It uses its strong claws to dig the eggs out of their nest, and then it gobbles them up.

A Crocodile's Day

 6:00 AM The Sun was just beginning to rise. I felt very sleepy and slow and needed to warm up in the Sun.

 7:00 AM Many animals came to the river to drink, but I didn't need to hunt. I ate a young antelope yesterday, and that filled me up!

 8:00 AM It was getting warmer. I called my hatchlings. They crawled on my back to hitch a ride. I looked for a sheltered riverbank where we could sunbathe.

 10:00 AM The Sun felt warm on my back. My little hatchlings played in the shallows. I warned them to stay close. Hungry predators always look for an easy meal.

 12:00 NOON The Sun was overhead, and I was too hot. I slid into the water to cool off.

2:00 PM I spotted a fish eagle swooping to pick up a fish. I called my hatchlings close and slapped the water with my big tail. I don't want my babies to be a snack for an eagle!

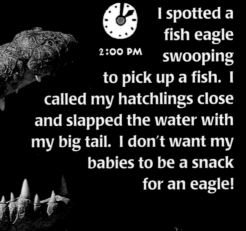

 **3:00 PM** The afternoon was peaceful, so I rested in the shallows and drifted off to sleep.

 4:00 PM I woke up hungry. It was time to find food. I stayed very still and waited.

 5:00 PM Only my eyes and nostrils showed above the water. A warthog walked toward the river. As it began to drink, I lunged. Snap! I pulled it down.

 8:00 PM It took me a long time to eat my supper. My hungry hatchlings fed on some of the smaller pieces of meat that dropped into the water as I ate.

 10:00 PM I sank lower in the muddy water. After the Sun set, the night turned cold. My hatchlings stayed close to me.

 4:00 AM It is very quiet in this sheltered part of the river. I'm still full from my feast last night, but I'm feeling cold. I am glad the Sun will rise soon.

Relatives

About twenty-two kinds of crocodiles, alligators, caimans, and gavials are in a group of reptiles called crocodilians. Crocodilians live in water and have lizard-shaped bodies, four legs, and long tails. They have not changed much since they developed about 200 million years ago.

Grinning Gavial!

The gavial, or gharial, lives in big rivers in southern Asia and grows to be 16 feet (5 m) long. It cannot move easily on land, but it is a great swimmer. It spends most of its time in the river and mainly eats fish. A gavial has a long, thin snout, which helps it catch fast fish. Its teeth fit together tightly, like a zipper. Even the slipperiest fish cannot escape the gavial's grip.

BIG AL!

American alligators live in the rivers and swamps of the southeastern United States. They eat fish, waterbirds, and anything else they can catch. They even grab farm animals and dogs if they get a chance!

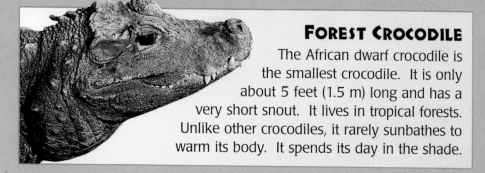

FOREST CROCODILE

The African dwarf crocodile is the smallest crocodile. It is only about 5 feet (1.5 m) long and has a very short snout. It lives in tropical forests. Unlike other crocodiles, it rarely sunbathes to warm its body. It spends its day in the shade.

CRAFTY CAIMAN

A caiman lives in swamps, lakes, and rivers in Central and South America. It eats anything from fish to deer.

Humans and Crocodiles

Crocodiles are the biggest and most feared of the reptiles on Earth today. They are the last living connection to the great group of reptiles that ruled the world at the time of the dinosaurs. Some of these reptiles may have been up to 50 feet (15 m) long and may have been the models for the dragons in fairy tales. Now, humans move onto the land where crocodiles live and hunt them for meat and skins. Some kinds of crocodiles are endangered.

DID YOU KNOW?

- The ancient Egyptians had a crocodile god called Sobek who was both admired and feared. Some crocodiles were kept and believed to be **sacred**. When they died, they were **mummified** and buried in special cemeteries.

- The ancient Romans wrestled with crocodiles in their circuses.

- Some traditional African people thought that wearing a crocodile tooth or claw would help keep them safe from attacks by crocodiles.

CROCODILE FARMING

Many kinds of crocodiles have been hunted for so long that they are rare in the wild. Now, hunting is illegal in parts of the world, but it could be too late. Many Nile crocodiles once lived in Egypt, but none live there now. In some places, crocodiles are raised on special farms for their meat and their skin. The skin, or hide, is made into bags, belts, boots, and other goods. Farming crocodiles can help protect the wild ones.

Glossary

ADAPTATIONS
Changes that a living thing goes through that allow it to better fit into the place where it lives.

BURROW
A tunnel or hole in the ground used as a shelter by an animal.

GUT
An animal's inside organs that digest food.

HATCHLINGS
Animals that have recently hatched.

MAMMALS
Warm-blooded animals that have backbones and have hair or fur on their skin and that feed their young with milk made in the mothers' bodies.

MARSHES
Areas of low land that are usually very wet.

MOLT
To shed an outer covering of skin, hair, or feathers.

MUMMIFIED
Treated with chemicals to preserve the body and prevent decay.

PREDATORS
Animals that hunt other animals for food.

PREY
Animals that another animal hunts and kills for food.

REEDS
Tall grasses that have hollow stems and grow in or near water.

REPTILE
A cold-blooded animal that has a backbone, crawls or walks on short legs, and produces its young by laying eggs.

SACRED
Holy or related to religion and treated with care and respect by believers.

SNOUT
A long nose that sticks out from the front of an animal's head.

TERRITORY
A large area of land claimed by someone or something for a particular use.

TROPICAL
Related to the hot, rainy part of Earth that is located near the equator.

INDEX

African dwarf crocodiles 27
alligators 8, 10, 22, 26, 27

caimans 10, 26, 27
claws 18, 23, 29

dinosaurs 11, 28

ears 8, 9
egg teeth 16
eggs 16, 22, 23
enemies 19, 22
eyes 8, 9, 20, 25

farms 27, 29
fighting 16
food 8, 13, 14, 17, 19, 20,
  21, 25

gavials 10, 26

hatchlings 16, 17, 21, 22,
  24, 25
humans 22, 28, 29
hunting 8, 10, 22, 23, 24,
  28, 29

jaws 6, 8, 16, 21, 22

lakes 10, 20, 27
legs 6, 7, 19, 26
lizards 6, 22, 26

marshes 10, 12
mouths 8, 16, 19, 20, 22

nests 16, 22, 23
Nile crocodiles 6, 10, 12,
  17, 18, 29
nostrils 8, 9, 20, 25

predators 8, 13, 20, 22, 24
prey 8, 9, 12, 20, 21,
  22, 23

reptiles 6, 11, 16, 26, 28
rivers 6, 10, 12, 16, 17, 18,
  20, 24, 25, 26, 27

saltwater crocodiles 11
skin 6, 16, 17, 20, 22,
  28, 29
snouts 9, 16, 18, 27
sunbathing 18, 19, 24, 27

tails 6, 7, 19, 24, 26
teeth 6, 8, 9, 20, 26, 29